SCATTERED AT SEA

SCATTERED AT SEA

AMY GERSTLER

PENGUIN POETS

PENGUIN BOOKS

Published by the Penguin Group
Penguin Group (USA) LLC
375 Hudson Street
New York, New York 10014

USA | Canada | UK | Ireland | Australia |
New Zealand | India | South Africa | China
penguin.com
A Penguin Random House Company

First published in Penguin Books 2015

Page xi constitutes an extension of this copyright page.

Illustrations by Gail Swanlund.

LIBRARY OF CONGRESS CATALOGING-IN-PUBLICATION DATA
Gerstler, Amy.
[Poems. Selections]
Scattered at sea / Amy Gerstler.
pages ; cm.—(Penguin poets)
ISBN 978-0-14-312689-8 (paperback)
I. Title.
PS3557.E735A6 2015
811'.54—dc23
2015002411

Printed in the United States of America
1 3 5 7 9 10 8 6 4 2

Set in Baskerville MT Std
Designed by Ginger Legato

He who obtains has little. He who scatters has much.

—Lao Tzu

CONTENTS

Poems in this book appeared, sometimes in slightly different forms, in the following periodicals, so thanks to these publications: *AGNI, The American Poetry Review, The Baffler, BODY, Catch Up, Columbia Poetry Review, Court Green, Eleven Eleven, MiPOesias, NAP, New Ohio Review, The New Republic, Plume, Poet Lore, Poetry, Poetry International, Salt Hill, Southern California Review,* and *Sou'wester.*

"Womanishness" appeared in *The Best American Poetry 2013,* guest-edited by Denise Duhamel, with series editor David Lehman. Thanks to both editors.

Special gratitude to the great artist and writer Benjamin Weissman, as well as Bernard Cooper, Dorna Khazeni, David Lehman, Dinah Lenney, Brighde Mullins, Michael Ryan, Paul Slovak, Gail Swanlund, David Trinidad, Irina Tsoy, and Brian Tucker.

SCATTERED AT SEA

I. KISSING

SEA FOAM PALACE

I.

Pardon this frontal offensive,
dear chum. Forgive my word-
churn, my drift, the ways this
text message has gotten all frothy.
How was it you became holy
to me? Should I resist, furiously?
Is this your true visage, shaken free,
glimpses of what underlies
the world we can see? *Do not
forget me* murmurs something
nibbled by fishes under the sea.

II.

I love the way you wear
your face, how you ride this life.
I delight in the sight of your
nervous, inquisitive eyes,
though I try to act otherwise.
Being stoned out of thy mind
only amps up thy fearsome
brain wattage. After dark
you're quicksilvery: wet/
slick/glistening. Don't make
me chase you, dragging
my heavy caresses, a pair of
awkward, serrated claws.
Some of us (but not you)

are poorly moored
to our bodies. We can
barely walk a straight line,
feeling every moment
just resuscitated
after having almost drowned,
still dribbling clear fluid
from the corners of our
mouths. We stagger
and shudder as buckets
of blood or semen or chocolate
mousse or spittle or lymph
or sludge sluice continually
through us. We bubble
and spume, trying
to talk underwater.

III.

Give me a swig of whatever
you're drinking, to put me
in tune with the cosmos'
relentless melt, with the rhythms
of dish-washing, corn-shucking,
hard-fucking, bed-wetting, and
folding the bones of other loves
into well-dug graves . . . may they
never become lost to the world.

EROTIC PSALM

That I may love this living, and you, till the end.

That I may peer into your body's holiest alcoves

and be kindled at first but a little by this,

then more hotly, stickily, sweetly,

licking at freckles, blemishes, scars

shame aims to keep under wraps but happily

can't. If god can't find a hole to enter us by

he will make one. Offer every blessed orifice,

then, every wet threshold, to beckon him in?

DEBRIS TRAIL

The world hikes up her skirts and her
underthings are so lovely! Lingerie dazzling
and jagged as a frozen waterfall, complete
with swallowed uproar. When you gesture,
my friend, your hand leaves a wake of gilded
images, subtle in coloration, and one hungers
to become, oh, everyone. I'd like to be you,
for example, just for a while, were it granted
me to test-drive being a man, to shoplift your
knowledge of ships, your passion for math,
your ecstatic, drug-addled past. Things go
solarized and velvety when you're superhigh,
right? Ancient explanations arise, and torchlit
processions. Currents of mercy singe rims
of each cup and leaf. I want to emit yips of love
while being refined in that fire, right by your side,
to lie flat on my back as meteors scorch the night
sky, both of us godseared, weeping, struck dumb.

PREHISTORIC PORN FILM

thighs sticky, leakage streaked
matted fur, meaty reek
grooming ruse—she has fleas
his hair stinks of burnt dirt
spectral whiffs of afterbirth
twig crack, muzzle cuff
snufflinglicks nuzzleshove
pinned down, kicking, legs entwining
mulchscuffle, bitemarks, whining
genitals' wild dialect
slick dizzy intersect
changing forms: tusks and horns
and beaks are seen at seizure's peak
jerking squirt, quickly spent
(kissing's not invented yet)

KISSING

Kissing occurs in skirmishes, wallops, or big gulps.

Pressing lips to lips or lips to objects jolts both souls.

Is kissing particular to mammals? Have you watched lizards or insects kiss?

Can you imagine kissing our grave, bearded waiter?

This kiss delivers a long-awaited verdict.

Kissing maps a hazardous passage.

Kissing offers prayers on deliverance from danger, or a prelude to wounding.

Two people kiss at the bottom of a lake, silt swirling around them.

Kissing grips kissers as the coldest winter on record gripped Europe.

Kissing makes plain the body's resolve.

Kissing references a text that no longer exists, which we try to conjure back
    into existence by kissing.

A SANE LIFE

Leaf skeletons everywhere,
denuded wings. Faces one itches
to kiss bob by every few seconds,
but one must restrain oneself or risk
imprisonment. They're all yakking
on cell phones, anyway, humming
"You'll Never Walk Alone" under their
precious, measured breaths.
Insured to the hilt, have you any
desire to be thought of in your
grave? To see your visage gracing,
say, the ten-dollar bill? To chuck
all devices and live on crackers,
molasses, and the occasional tastily
prepared bug? To slosh your toxicity
outside the alembic of self, just to see
how acidic it is? To disentangle
each task's tentacles from around
your scrawny neck? *Relax responsibly*
a beer ad urges. And that means
while blitzed on our hoppy product
do no harm? We swallow sunlight
in pills, outlive our wits, and ultimately
get shunted off to rest homes tended
by underpaid strangers. Clean food
costs more than the poisoned kind.
Soft, tasteful clothes in natural-dyed
hues (paprika, cinnabar, and almond)
cost more than the bright, starch-stiff

ones also made by slaves.
SALE ON PREFAB YURTS!
My opponent's attitude toward
planet Earth seems to be simply
Good riddance! Come to think of it,
dispensing random, impulse-driven
kisses might be just the ticket, a great
campaign strategy, worth a day
or two in the clink. A friend
with inside dope says every cell
downtown's got color TV. He claims
our local jailers make great pizza.

FALL ON YOUR KNEES

On waking, if seized by an urge to munch shrubs,
give in. Swing your legs over the lee side of the bed.
(What self-appointed princess owns these pink velvet
slippers?) Tromp into the garden and graze while you
may. Chew dew-bejeweled weeds till they complain,
Rivers will swallow you, stupid human, for turning them to syrup.
Thirsty birds, who flicker in huge eucalyptus, how will
you punish us? Coffee, ignite my coward mind, ever
ready to flee. Make her stay. Or at least let me see her
again. Fellow men, let your leaky perfection spur me
to worship as you bash galvanized cans in symphonic
impact this trash day. Speak to me sweetly of adversity's
value. And you, gaggle of errant selves, flock of motley
buzzards, population ever-changing, scavenge that crash
site, this bed, as I sip this morning's cocktail, an eye-opener
after last night's revels: bitters mixed with curds of cloud.

IN SEARCH OF SOMETHING TO WORSHIP, MY EYES LIGHTED ON YOU

Wizened was he, body and soul,
even in youth. I'm drawn to men
life has sledgehammered,
sucker punched, and their
faces' rocky topography.
From our first meeting his visage
was familiar to me. Other faces
formed and burst beneath his roughed-up
public one, surfacing like battered cargo
post-shipwreck, or like alternative verdicts
rising in the minds of a tired jury,
or like the stowaway radiance that shone
through his clothes—yes, I said *radiance*,
though he was mostly composed
of unbuffered fury and sorrow,
fermenting like moonshine within
his body's rickety still. Years later,
he needed to leap, throw himself
from some parapet into the arms
of a confident virgin. Now he's the
invisible guest at all my feasts.
Despite having built a cult around
that man, complete with amulets, altars,
censors, and shrines, despite
my swallowed knowledge, my compliant
defiance, I could not save him.

II. WOMANISHNESS

WOMANISHNESS

The dissonance of women. The shrill frilly silly
drippy prissy pouty fuss of us. And all the while
science was the music of our minds. Our sexual
identities glittery as tinsel, we fretted about god's
difficulties with intimacy, waiting for day's luster
to fade so we could slip into something less
venerated. Like sea anemones at high tide
our minds snatched at whatever rushed by.
Hush, hush, my love. These things happened
a long time ago. You needn't be afraid of them, now.

THOUGHTS OF TREES AT TWILIGHT

Distant trees are first to blacken,
silent as druids or choked-back vows.
Back at the house, pillars dimly
mimic them. Some trunks glow copper,
like girls' arms raised in balletic gesture,
which brings a lump to the throat. How
long will the girls these trees worship
(and by whom they are worshipped
in turn) be this vulnerable, this pitiless,
amidst symphonies of orchards,
the year's last windfall apples heaped
in bruised tribute at their feet?

BON COURAGE

Why are the woods so alluring? A forest appears
to a young girl one morning as she combs
the dreams from her hair. The trees rustle
and whisper, shimmer and hiss. The forest
opens and closes, a door loose on its hinges,
banging in a strong wind. Everything in the dim
kitchen—the basin, the jug, the skillet, the churn—
snickers scornfully. In this way a maiden
is driven toward the dangers of a forest,
but the forest is our subject, not this young girl.

She's glad to lie down with trees towering all around.
A certain euphoria sets in. She feels molecular,
bedeviled, senses someone gently pulling her hair,
tingles with kisses she won't receive for years.
Three felled trees, a sort of chorus, narrate
her thoughts, or rather channel theirs through her,
or rather subject her to their peculiar verbal
restlessness: . . . *our deepening need for nonbeing* intones
the largest, most decayed tree, midsentence.
I'm not one of you squeaks the battered sapling,

blackened by lightning. Their words become metallic
spangles shivering the air. *Will I forget the way home?*
the third blurts. *Why do I feel like I'm hiding in a giant's nostril?*
the oldest prone pine wants to know. *Are we being freed
from matter?* the sapling asks. *Insects are well intentioned,*

offers the third tree, by way of consolation. *Will it grow impossible to think a thought through to its end?* gasps the sapling, adding in a panicky voice, *I'm becoming spongy!* The girl feels her hands attach to some distant body. She rises to leave, relieved these trees are not talking about *her*.

CURSING OF THE PARTY RESPONSIBLE FOR HER SUFFERING

May his scalp sizzle, blister, and itch.

May his nose run like the Amazon.

May his lips swell to melons.

May his tongue bubble with eruptions.

May he choke as though he had swallowed a pitchfork.

May his stomach combust.

May his genitals resemble a witch's pinkie and two shriveled peas.

May he be unable to find his feet.

May his bones turn to dough.

May his mind drown in the slop of which his soul is composed.

ON WANTING TO BE MALE

Craved the swagger more than the rod. (Is that true?) Lusted after their sprint speed, briefcases, Tahitian aftershave, crew cuts, blue nuts, thrusty cutlasses. Fascinated by (but not covetous of) their crepey ball-skin, crenulated like brains, or walnut hulls, or iguana hide on a rich dude's shoes. Was awed by every lunge, parry, and feint of the sword of a thousand truths. The female model comes equipped with undulating, oft-colonized potential baby cave (that dark Carlsbad Cavern wherein blindfish may swim), mysterious even to many women sitting on it.

SELF-PORTRAIT AS CAVE LADY

Nameless volcanoes vomit rock.
Can't keep cave clean. Swarms
of striped flies invade at dusk, bats
catch too few. Tender feeling for
baby mammoth as we eat him.
Sudden juice-leak from my eyes.
I pet baby mammoth's roasted
hide, unfold hairy earflap still
stuck to skull and whisper into it.
Later, take chips of burnt sticks,
spit, plus mammoth fat, mix
in cup of hand and use paste I
make to sketch young mammoth
on shadow wall. Make black hand-
prints too. Rub mammoth fat
on my old, cracked feet. Rub some
on scars. Gather fresh, dry leaves
for sleep. Give baby chunk of tusk
to suck so he'll shut up. His yowls
rile wolves, who pace and whine
just beyond the all-night fires.

MERRYTHOUGHT

"No," I corrected the rosy-cheeked nurse,
"*I* am the wife and *she* is his mistress." He died
stoned out of his mind, as we wept farewells
and caressed the thin white harelip scar con-
necting his left nostril to bristly upper lip.
Now he's part of *that which always is,* survived by
me and my shy sister-in-crimes of trampled
convention. Well, not *trampled,* exactly, more
like *polka-ed upon.* Some days I'm almost a man,
barking harsh laughs, my anger an incandescent
brand of valor. The sight of this slight woman,
auburn hair fanned out on pillows, is enough
to flush floods of hummingbirds from the aviary
just beneath my stomach. And boy, those
hummingbirds are HUNGRY! The reckless
joys of maidenhood uppermost in our minds,
we made lists during bedside vigils, while he
drifted, of things we could do together, besides
sex, after the man in whose clasp we had melded
was gone. Then we each kissed his wishbone
(his neck smelled of peasant-y bread) and left
him forever, to the grave ministrations of this
raven-haired young nurse, now orphaned,
whose touch he had loved so much.

PALE QUEEN

Her sovereignty. Your poverty. Her mocha-
nippled majesty. All her faults, those small
assaults. Her kisses, which taste of ancient faiths.
Pray don't reproach her, imprisoned as she is
in her latest incarnation, dazed by pent-up
scents that waft from her hair as she unwinds it
at night. When she asks, "Do I look like a harlot
in this dress?" insist that's ridiculous. When she
inquires if pin curls make her a dead ringer
for some medieval Spanish rabbi, better not
laugh if you value This Unnatural, Utterly
Lovely Woman, who drowned her child in a pond
five lives ago, such was the distracted state
of her mind: *I cannot pray, and can never repent . . .*

CHILDLESSNESS

The past wafts its melodies into the future
through a promising youngster with a talent for music.
Intoxicating, the smell of a baby's neck,
and the fat little askings of infant hands.
Is a child an exegesis of parental texts?
(This medicine must be drunk right after sex.)
His favorite book is *A Child's Garden of Ruins and Wrecks.*

A man's sweat can get you pregnant. Beware.
Women have been fertilized by animal bites, dreams,
swallowing insects, seawater, eating beans.
Yet love will not swell her useful womb.
"The whisper of dry leaves being crushed
underfoot and kisses blown to the blessed dead
are all I leave behind," she said.

III. DUST OF HEIRS,
DUST OF ANCESTORS

ANCESTOR PSALM

So who are your people, anyway? Freud?
The Marx Brothers? Kafka? Anne Frank?
Thick-lipped, Brillo-haired Jews
in smoky brown photos. Girls whose
hair bows, giant butterflies, flap back
to the Schwarzwald at night. Grandpa's
list of solemn mistresses in bobbed hair
and furs, floppy cloth flowers pinned
to their collars. A squinty infant gripping
a pear. Squishy-faced babies in lace dresses.
Grandma in seed pearls. An uncle,
cap like a fallen soufflé, cutting
wool for winter coats. And this babushka
lady, face so like a potato I *know* we're
related. Black shawl, long striped skirt,
heavy black shoes, double-chinned
peasant mug, hands stubby as ginger
roots, just like mine. Madame Tuberinsky
(I must address you thus, for I'll
never know your real name),
generous lender of DNA: How long
did you drink the milk of the world?
Did god's eyes open and close and
suddenly your life was done? Can you
offer me any hope at all? None? *None?*

DI$CLAIMER

Though unmoored and fearful in spirit,
    you, trembling investor,
        rather than ourselves or our affiliates,
            will incur the bulk of the risk
               the bulk of the punishment

The value of your investments may fluctuate
    as psychotics' moods do

If you meet minimum suitability requirements
    if your miracle bra lifts your assets' value
        if our strategic partners emerge from the loving embrace of their regulators

        you may then be eligible . . .

though there is no guarantee of any level of return on your investment
    no assurance your entire investment will not be lost
        or that it won't ultimately fund some hand's hunger for scepter or weapon

We trust you have read:
    the Trading with the Enemy Act
        the Sad Proxy Documents
            the Alternative Realities Declaration
                the Specially Designated Global Terrorist Checklist
                    the Multiple Minds of God Adjustments
                        the Foreign Narcotic$ Kingpin De$ignation
                          and the Unacceptable, Sweaty, Crestfallen Investor
                              Dialectic—

Right now, nobody has reliable data in any of these fields, so

   we can provide no assurances

      based on current expectations, plans, estimates, projections, or fuzzy, globular masses of feeling, which represent incompletely processed and more or less melted childhood dreams and beliefs

         provided by blinkered individuals beyond our control
who may splatter your lap with liquidity events

We may not be able to raise substantial funds
   without feasting on
      portion-controlled steaks daily
         as well as full-bodied single-malt scotches
            with rose-gold highlights
               the costs of which would be passed along to you

Our officers face significant conflicts of interest as the drug wears off

This is considered a "blind pool" offering. Therefore, you may see flashes of orange and yellow when tired. The corners of your eyes may fill with a milky discharge. You may see pulsating bars in your peripheral vision at times, especially when there are sudden changes in illumination, and thus you may not be able to adequately evaluate our ability to achieve investment objectives

If your reality is so vibrant and exciting, *fool,*

if you're so almighty high-minded,

then simply *give your wealth away*

for the purposes of this document, the words "we," "us,"
   and the phrase "ourselves or our affiliates"
     refer to the lives of the pious
             for whom all things turn out for the best

Certain categories of purchasers
   who take an unscheduled doze at a crucial moment
     will incur hefty exit fees

ON BUYING A WALKER

Amble is what she can't do anymore.
Not step, stroll, or promenade.
Not without aid. Hence this errand
at summer's height. A solo drive
to the Valley, after research online,
to buy a model:

> Equipped with deluxe padded seat and padded backrest
> Plus lightweight aluminum frame
> Previously owned or new
> Available in rose, silver, or blue

Lord, why did I, an unathletic klutz,
sprint into the medical supply store
as if auditioning for the Olympics?
Not by design did I bust out running,
but by sudden, unanticipated instinct.
This contraption I'm about to buy isn't for me,
not yet! my shameless legs ached to say.
Inside, the air-conditioning was dialed
up so high it tousled my hair during
the transaction. A dwarf whose legs
didn't work sat astride a top-of-the-line
motorized scooter, chatting with his
able-bodied friend. Friend allowed
as how he liked my hibiscus print dress.
As my now-nonambulatory mother
had drummed into me for my entire
speaking life, I said *thanks* in response

to the compliment. My mother, whose
mobility's diminished to such an extent
that she cries out for joy finding a stray
shopping cart in the street because she
can lean on it as she hobbles along,
her once lovely body too damaged to heft.
Hence this errand. God, this is your theft.

ANCIENT CHINESE PHILOSOPHY

If she were an ancient
Chinese philosopher
she'd contemplate lotuses
afloat on Echo Park Lake
each one like a cupped hand
and she'd compose verses
on braiding a neighbor's hair
and on her son's fear of small dogs
and on rubbing honey into cuts
that don't easily heal
and on revelatory smells
a man's body releases in sleep
like iron rusting in rainwater
and on how every word ever spoken
from darkest antiquity till now yes
the past of all humanity
reverberates in an unheard-
by-human-mortals chorus
a relentless crescendo
birds and other animals can hear
which is lately perceived
by those sensitive fellow beings
as an insistent warning roar

THE DEAD WOMAN'S TELEPHONE

Hello, I'm Jewish,
is a playful way
to answer the dead
woman's telephone.
*What happened to all
the Jews in Poland?*
demands a gravelly
voice on the dead
woman's telephone.
Should one wear
a poppy in one's lapel
when placing a call
from the dead
woman's telephone?
Voice mail retrieved
from the dead
woman's telephone:
*Yes, yes, the Jews.
We were sorry
to see them go.
They made rose petal
marmalade. They gave
babies poppy seed tea
to make them sleepy.*
The rumble of pogroms
is heard while falling
asleep, ear resting
on the receiver
of the dead

woman's telephone.
Light sluices
into the room as a
female police officer,
on the ninth or tenth
ring, picks up the dead
woman's telephone
and jerks open her
curtains. You must be
resolutely on the side
of the lowly
to hear all that's said
on the dead
woman's telephone.
Proposals concerning
the relocation
of the forsaken
are now being received
via the dead
woman's telephone.

A SHORT HISTORY OF SUBLIME MOMENTS ON HOLD

Press one if you'd like to speak to Attila the Hun.

Press two if your Jacuzzi is filled with eels.

Press three if bitten by an animal you teased while it was eating.

Press four if being heartsore dulls you to the delights of this world.

Press five to put continents between you and a thriving former love.

Press six if your whiskey "fix" (that floaty limbo following on the heels of your
initial sip) is the high point of your day.

Press seven to hear actor Kevin Bacon explain the limbic system.

Press eight to be connected to an invertebrate.

Press nine to explore origins of the phrase "time out of mind."

Press ten to listen to Neanderthal bone-flute music (again).

EARLY GREEK PHILOSOPHY

One imagines them still tangled in half-naked grapplings
With their half-magic world in which stones have souls
In which plants feel nude and ashamed when their leaves are torn off
In which Earth's afloat in some cosmic amniotic broth
    like a log in a stream
In which suns and moons exist without limit
In which attempts are made to explain monstrous births
In which everything is teeming with god(s)
Some pundits believe these Greeks
Invented explanation and the art of argument
(Along with the Persians, Egyptians, Africans
[Yes! Black Athena!!] Italians, plus many other
Cultures these hungry Greeks sucked up)
Their syncretized world squeezed into being
By a sequence of green individuals
All sporting curly beards
Who totally got off on criticizing each other
On observing eclipses
On sorting the jumble of events into gorgeous order
Getting a lot of the science right
While still pawing through entrails to divine the future
A vigorous lot of intellectual adventurers
Whose mission was to explain the universe
Wild minds we have only in fragments
Because whether papyrus scraps, birch bark
Or this mortal coil
Dammit, matter just doesn't last

ELIJAH, DEAD PROPHET, ROAMS THE EARTH

judgmental and zealous
his guts rubble
his beard a pale exhalation
a version of Elijah
(how we like to taste his name!)
appears in the Qur'an
and on this particular holiday
Elijah's invited inside
Jews' doors propped open
cups of wine placed
on crocheted tablecloths
for his spirit to drink
tonight Elijah prowls the house
of a man widowed twice
rifles the sleeping family's
belongings: letters and bills
schoolbooks and shoes
he examines their trash
coffee grounds orange peels
an empty Band-Aid tin
the widower and sons snore
their dog lifts her head
drums her tail and smiles at Elijah
the youngest boy wakes convinced
something sat astride him all night
whispering about being fed
by ravens in a cave
when the boy rises he feels sick
as if an organ had been removed

while he slept but after some milk
after worried inquiries from Dad
the boy shakes off his malaise and
when he thinks no one is looking
the widower chugs Elijah's wine
no sense letting it go to waste
it tastes like dirt from the cellar floor
like tree bark like the inside
of a woman's mouth
Elijah lived a mysterious life
he raised the dead
brought fire from the sky
foretold people's fates
was taken up in a whirlwind
and reached the quiet stars
whose weariness it is said
pervades all creation

STOICS

Let the dogs run the wet meadow.
Philosophers say we're made of fire

and smolder all our lives. Mustn't grumble
upmappable sadness, they warn, at scouring pads

of gray cloud abrading the night sky.
Whining turns the brain to molasses.

Rich food hampers the intellect.
Regret clogs arteries. We stuff ourselves

with bread and sex. Then ash provides
the most natural last transport

imaginable. No need for granite slabs
or silk-lined coffins. The dogs, to whom

you are too passionately attached,
ignore your bright lies

(which have reached critical
mass), absorbed as they are

in chasing rabbits across the drenched field,
while the garrulous world drones on and on.

IV. WHAT I DID WITH YOUR ASHES

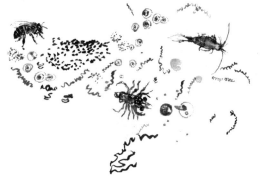

THE SUICIDE'S WIFE

lives on an island
of last-ditch attempts
and ancient consolations

after the shipwreck
she swam ashore near naked
hands scraped raw on coral
bra and panties soaked through
sand in her teeth
lapped by aftermath
lying exhausted
slowly approaching
the condition of music

he loved her stubborn luster
sure they argued sometimes
the word "argue" from Latin
meaning *to make clear*
while she sat quietly
in the wing chair
her eyes closed
police ransacked his desk
the note turned up in his pocket
with the letter for his sister
a baseball ticket stub
receipts for two "taco platters"
he whose soul was bound up with mine
and part of a bookmark

six weeks later she looks great
thin and translucent
a statue of justice sans blindfold
she wears beautiful blouses now
peach, gold, seedling green
her complexion
has never been better
lushness nips at the heels
of destruction

tonight's lurid sunset's
a cocktail of too many boozes
she'd like to switch it off
via remote control
but there's no antidote
for celestial events

a frantic bat takes a wrong turn
from the attic veers
into her living
room, bounces off walls
a sick *flut-thud* each time it hits
the suicide's wife
pulls out her roasting pan
climbs the kitchen counter
teeters and grabs
for twenty minutes
at last claps on the lid
walks her prize outside

releases the creature
into the trees
where the lawn peters out
where the idea that at death
something is liberated
can flap blackly away.

DEAR NATION OF MY DEAD,

Atheist Jews, seizure sufferers,
genius drunks, little brothers,
warblers of arias, cross-dressing shrinks,
old loves with viral appetites,
daughters and sons who never saw daylight,
hamsters and scrappy cats of my youth:
yeah, I'm mad. Crushed. Sniveling.
Conscripted by myth, you're smug, triumphant.
Nature dutifully scatters your essences,
dramatic, illegible. So what's a sentient
being to do, marooned on this barstool,
but slurp, savor, summon, and pray, as I
sop up this gravy with hunks of warm sourdough
torn from this morning's glowing loaf?

EXTRACTS FROM THE CONSOLER'S HANDBOOK

sleepless grief
rises quietly
twice a night
to change its soaked
pajamas

a fist lodged in its throat
submissive grief
sips the offered broth
but spits into a napkin
the minute you look away

after fucking in the underbrush
jealous fury and voracious grief
walk slowly home
in opposite directions
their hair full of dead leaves

impatient grief
braids and unbraids
the tablecloth fringe
taps out Morse code
with its loafer toe
sending messages
to the newly dead
the body's a bear trap
while enduring the fat pastor's
kindly insights and pouring him
more coffee

root cellar grief
burrows in a crawl space
beneath its former home
never wipes its feet and mounts
the stairs into the well-lit house
where casseroles featuring
melted cheese are being reheated
and children are having their baths

in volcanic grief
the sufferer never again
enjoys life aright till the lava
has cooled and taken on
wondrous blackened forms

soul-wandering grief
no longer recognizes proper conduct
the wicked are dear to it
with the virtuous it finds no delight

long past midnight
solitary grief
may be briefly relieved
by the loud sounds
of lively mice
banging around
inside a cold stove

HE SLEEPS EVERY AFTERNOON,

rimless glasses askew, chin on chest, for a few hours. Actually, he dozes most of the day. Book on his lap where a fig leaf might be. Marc likes to stretch out on his long green couch under the picture window. Perched near his sneakered feet, his ginger cat naps or sits motionless, slowly opening and closing her eyes. A conscientious sentry, she'll desert her post only to leap to the window ledge when birds throng the feeder right outside. She'll stare through the glass, making a guttural rasp, like someone saying "ack! ack! ack!" Birds ignore the agitated feline but disperse when it begins to snow.

Marc's looking younger than thirty. Aging backward, as hibernators sometimes do. Later, I'll wake him, give him lunch and a shave. The razor clears paths through shaving cream like the town plow clearing snow.

Once I was kindly disposed toward all deities. Osiris, Helios, Odin, Buddha, Anansi, Sita, Athena, Baal. They seemed romantic to me. I wanted to know their attributes, special powers, and imaginative backstories. Now the whole inscrutable crew has lost my vote. Outside, fields of parched prairie grass rattle. Mountain lions, seldom seen, keep local rodents in check. It's clear and cold here. You can see for miles, unlike where I come from, a sprawling, temperate city so smoggy that nearby mountains are visible only after a three-day rain.

Marc's closest neighbors complain deer nibble their garden to nubs. A buck and his harem are grazing there now. The husband of this neighbor couple pees around the perimeter of their large garden at night, as the scent of human urine is said to repel deer.

Marc's mind's now a suitcase packed by a clown. Sometimes he rummages around and pulls out the striped sock or folding travel clock he was looking for. Other times, he'll dig up a surprise: a rubber snake, a string tie he doesn't remember owning, a spatula. He wakes, sets his book facedown on the floor. "I'm lounging in these chairs watching a curtain-to-curtain preview," he tells me. *That must be fun* is the best I can do. "Everybody in this neighborhood is at least a five!" he says enthusiastically. *At the very least!* I agree. I'm making him macaroni and cheese, stirring white sauce with a whisk. The cat jumps onto his legs. He yanks her tail gently and she head-butts his arm. "The other cat is being nostalgic, cause he's wheezing like he was admiring me as a child," he tells me, before nodding off. There is no other cat. Not quite time for pain medication.

I kneel on the not very clean floor beside the couch and stare at his stubbly face as he sleeps. The cat turns up her purr volume, revving the pleasure engine, expecting me to pet her. Marc's hands twitch energetically. That's new. *It's still him*, I tell myself every day. *Still alive. Still in there.* His sense of humor is mostly intact. He recognizes me. He knows who he is. Remembers many recent events. Except for the staples in his scalp he looks great.

ON THE IDEA THE DEAD MAY LIVE VICARIOUSLY THROUGH US

gravestones
that vanished
a century ago
now reappear

perpetual loneliness flows
from century to century
from mosque
to churchyard
to synagogue

the living ferment
what our dead were
before immersion

our dead remain forces
we believe ourselves
at the mercy of
  today's
        brain fizz
        musty hungers
        raw longing

as we plunge
from moral
or fiscal cliffs
our dead tumble
with us

children tear pages
from a large-format atlas
to make kites
our dead delight in
that harsh purr
each page makes
ripping away
they crave
ragged edges

you tire easily
the dead have been sipping
your present bloom
your present perfection
they flicker
and bicker
inside you at night

what shall remain
of the hand-me-down earth
for the meek to claim
when lovers of blood sport
have finished with it
only a welling up
that last gasp:
vapor of vapors

WHAT I DID WITH YOUR ASHES

Shook the box like a maraca.

Stood around like a dope in my punch-colored dress, clutching your box to my chest.

Opened your plastic receptacle, the size of a jack-in-the-box. But instead of gaudy stripes, your box is sober-suit blue, hymnal blue.

Tasted them. You've gained a statue's flavor, like licking the pyramids, or kissing sandstone shoulders. I mean *boulders*.

Remarked to your box: "REINCARNATION comes from roots meaning 'to be made flesh again.'"

Stowed your box under my bed for a week to seed dreams in which you advise me. (This didn't work.)

Opened the Babylonian Talmud at random. Read aloud to your gritty, gray-white powder: "There are three keys which the Holy One, blessed be He, has not entrusted into the hands of any messenger. These are: the key of rain, the key of birth, and the key of the resurrection of the dead." Worked myself up to watery eyes. Any intensity evaporated the instant I stopped reading.

Tried to intuit your format, sift it from tides of void. Does shape play a role? My watch ticked in an exaggerated way. Closed my eyes, sent forth mental tendrils seeking the nothing of you. They curled back on themselves, weaving around the wing chair, a dog's leg, a lamp stand, eventually heading back toward the nothing of me.

IT WAS A SPLENDID MIND

that now seemed shriveled, slightly.
What had she wanted to say?

Her brain's deglazing . . .
crispy bits of id,
and ego drippings,

he'd leave
his glasses on during sex,
declaring, "I need to see
your creamy meat!"

HER HAIR DID NOT APPEAR BRUSHED AND HER
CLOTHING WAS STAINED.

Longevity is the first of the five blessings.

Hi sweetie,
It looks like they want to medicate the shit out of her! This morning she refused help,
refused to walk with her cane. She won't let Elena put the medicated cream on her,
and she won't let me do it, either. She said she has been doing it herself (giant lie!).
She got very angry with me and said she wouldn't talk to me, only write me notes
from now on. That is where things stand. I am fed up but fine.

BOSTON NAMING TEST
GERIATRIC DEPRESSION SCALE
MATTIS DEMENTIA RATING SCALE, SECOND EDITION
VERBAL FLUENCY TEST
WECHSLER MEMORY SCALE, FOURTH EDITION
WISCONSIN CARD-SORTING TEST
CLOCK-DRAWING TEST

Shape cookies into numerals
representing the children's ages.
They will love it!!!

Does her bedroom smell
like a cave
in which ash-wrapped
cheeses are ripening?

PATIENT ASSERTS, "THINGS KEEP SLIDING OUT
OF MY HEAD."
(OCCASIONAL DISPOSITION TO WEEP.)

**Your mother threw these items at her Life-Enhancement
Assistant this morning:**

a small bottle of cologne
an empty pill caddy
a napkin ring in the shape of a snake

REMEMBER THESE THREE WORDS. YOU'LL BE ASKED TO
REPEAT THEM AT THE END OF THE TEST:
1. APPLE
2. TABLE
3. PENNY

A More Interesting Three-Item List:
1. throbbing kiss
2. kiss that awakens the blood
3. kiss that kindles love

As I explained to your sister today, your mother's behav-
ior is related to her diagnosis, and it needs to be controlled
chemically. She needs the right medication to control these
outbursts, like the one Wednesday when she ran out of the
house in her nightgown and tried to start the car.

Or even this list of desserts:
1. Charlotte Russe

2. baba au rhum

3. cherries jubilee

Hi sweetie,

After I got back from taking Lucas to practice, I had just gotten him in the tub when Mom called and said Elena was giving her the wrong pills. I went over and showed her that Elena was giving her the proper pills, but she thinks Elena is trying to poison her. This is hell. I need a drink.

Spirit glaze for ham:

½ cup dry red wine

1 cup bourbon whiskey

6 cloves

2 tbsp grated orange peel

¼ cup honey

bouquets and
bouquets of faces

yet this oblivion of names

Hi sweets,

Took Mom to the opera. After the performance found her in the ladies' room scrubbing her giant white underpants in the fancy marble sink, as though she was home.

Never refer to an elderly woman's genitals
as "dead, empty crater."
Address them instead as,
"Dear dormant volcano
containing a freshwater lake."

ON YOUR NEXT VISIT CAN YOU MAKE HER TAKE A BATH????!

Today is a holiday, but which one?
Thanksgiving? Valentine's Day?

How do you turn on the radio again?

I want to remind you that your mother is not safe to be left alone at home.

The Three Times He Carried Her:
1. across the threshold of their first apartment in Kensington in the rain
2. over the pebbly beach, laughing, into Lake Champlain
3. through the shushing hospital doors when her water broke

Her daughters with their conspiratorial air.
One strongly resembles her dead husband, the other not at all.
Her dead son stands with them in his purple basketball jersey. He asks,

What does the brain matter, compared with the heart?

Now she remembered what she had been going to say.

V. ONLY AT CERTAIN SACRED LOCATIONS

ACCOUNT OF FORMER LIVES

In one life I drank so hard I always had the spins
In another life I breast-fed several sets of twins
In one life blips of happiness
    kept me contented, more or less
In another I slurped wet harvests from between her thighs
In another I lived celibate, terrified, and disguised
In one life my head was full of catchy songs and dances
In another I got high on taking awful chances
In one life I was guillotined
In another I drank kerosene
In one life I stuttered
In another I regretted every word I ever uttered
In one life I fell from a ship's rigging
In another I was a scrawny boy obsessed with digging
In one life I had a painful case of housemaid's knee
In another all I ever wanted was to flee
In one life I accidentally blinded a child
In another I was soundly beaten and exiled
In one life I was a dandy with a wispy beard
In another I was a dullard who wept as sheep were sheared
In one life I was a monk who won a newborn in a bet
In this life Lord knows what is to happen yet

A TERRIBLY SENTIMENTAL FORK

As unmined silver
I spent eons in twilight sleep,
rubbed lustrous by seasons,
and learnt much from it.
Thumbless hand,
I've been jammed
into tine-bending clay
to gouge holes
for planting jasmine
when a spade wasn't handy.
Human mistreatment
of their best inventions
led this still-handsome fork
(my classic pattern's
known as *Acanthus*
or *Aegean weave*)
to be employed
prying up old linoleum.
Forks are mentioned
six times in the Bible!
Slave of the grip, bound
to spear earthworms
or currants, I have
pedigree, nobility,
but am sans volition.
Today, the brat
in the dotted Swiss pinafore,
plagued by frequent nosebleeds,
used me to stab the cat. I am

scholar, diplomat! Striving's
elongated shape! Yet my fate
is shame. As if pitched here
by some tantrum-prone
god, I've lain for days
in the grass where
I was flung.

MIRACULOUS,

that there was no blood in the toilet this morning.
That the beloved dog lasted as long as he did.
(His patience and resignation remain,
though you can no longer smell them.)
That waking ever follows hibernation:
truly astonishing. Incredible, that illness
is ever recovered from, that curtains so
faithfully translate the language of wind.

SASSAFRAS

Believing that *all* lakes are handsome,
the sassafras basks in fibrous silence.
Wrung from her brief hours and weeks,
sap weeps from graffiti incised
in the bark of the sassafras tree. Sassafras
leaves cure gonorrhea. The sassafras aspires
to a lightly psychedelic, ethical mind.
Will the sassafras rustle up
her spiritual autobiography,
confessions of blue fruit dropped
too soon, seeds ferried too far afield?
Tall and spreading, dependent on
rainfall variations, the sassafras grieves
felled cousins and extinct loves. *Let me
complete my years in happiness*, the sassafras pleads.
The sassafras, with her three distinct leaf
patterns, lives at peace with the deer and the bees.
Be not sad, sassafras tree, less impressive
than redwoods, less gaudy than maple,
less exotic than palms. God's wooden saints
wait patiently in a cold rain, not the least
of these being his high on disquiet,
soul-splintered sassafras tree.

PENANCE

As court-ordered punishment for theft
of a necklace, you're scrubbing morgue
floors. Not with your tongue, just this
dreadlocked mop. Outside, flies land
on banisters. Thanks, flies, for trying
to punctuate this out-of-control moment,
for attempts to insert necessary pauses
and prevent confusion. *Sigh.* Your
shoes are getting wet. Why does
the need to be high, to be lit from
within by urgent bursts, to feel noisy
hordes armed with flamethrowers
storming one's barricades—why
do these groveling wants never
cease? Why do they insist, "Party or
perish"? Why swipe what you could
easily buy? In your pocket's a letter,
delivered years late. An old love,
rinsed in religion by intervening
decades, begs you to forgive him.
Or did you only dream his apology
finally arrived on cream-colored
paper? Replies you could send him
by mental telegram: *Our department
of regrets isn't hiring right now, but you may
leave your résumé.* No. That's unkind.
Or: *I wish you the best, but I'm busy
making amends to this dingy linoleum.*
Let narratives of the past remain

murky, submerged. Let the lava-
encrusted fortress of your thoughts
stay mysteriously locked. Now empty your
bucket. Try, for once in your life, to really
wake up. Refill with clean, soapy water.

RUMBLES FROM A MINOR DEITY

"Thanks for the badass offering!

Enjoying your fat, juicy existence?

Please accept this omen index.

Leave off seeking what wounds you. I won't warn you again.

Weirdos are heroes: be not conformed to the world.

Don't let yourself go cruel around the mouth.

One should give light to the whole world,

And when that gets tiring, lie down on various gregarious grasses.

Every tinfoil-and-twine shrine hidden in some garage,

Every duct-taped shoebox of relics under a bed,

Every self-sprung temple circumscribed by sublime trees

And screeching monkeys: all these are dear to me.

As we wrap up this chat, I want you to know:

I'm only a couple of days of abject praying away . . ."

HOFFNUNG

He fancies his chances are good with her,
unaware that in the years since the war

she has come to prefer women whose cunts
taste like mustard. To pin one's hopes on

a bark-colored moth, its wings crinkled
like crepe paper, a moth affixed high

on the kitchen wall, frozen for days where
it will likely die in noble clinging mode

just under the cobwebby heating vent,
is to confirm your need for more friends

and a greater daily quota of sunlight.
To raise C.'s hopes that T. can stop

drinking and then to liken those
hopes to fields of undulating grain,

alfalfa perhaps, is to wish C. hip-deep
in acres of unscythed denial. The blind

typist hopes she'll be hired tonight without
her disability becoming an issue. L. said he felt

hope's rhizomes race through his body,
radiating in all directions, like some incipient

disease he'd been fighting since childhood.
Hope, he said, *it's as insidious as bitterness.*

If mother earth only knew how much we
loved one another she would creak, shudder,

and split like a macheted melon, releasing
the fiery ball of molten hope at her core.

KITCHEN ANNUNCIATION

And the Lord appeared to her
as she scraped dishes at the sink.
And the Lord mumbled in her ear:
  "Brute beast led by sensuality
  and yearning, weak as an earthworm,
  don't shun my light. Correct your
  affections. Revel while you're flesh.
  Make music in any fashion you can.
  Bow before the suicide's furious purpose.
  Protect your realm. Parry all thrusts
  and blows, if only with silence.
  Take advice from certain birds
  you admire. Neither a slacker
  nor self-contented be. Decide
  whether to keep mum re:
  this vision of me, of which, in a
  moment, no trace will remain."

GRATITUDE PRAYER

Thanks for the rickety body, which lends us form!
And for what we believe can't be scattered at sea.
Thanks for itinerant monks, enraged mobs,
And blind librarians! Thanks for mothers of ten,
Sticky little leaves, salt and frogs.
Thanks for alphabets freighted with vast
Past minds, for verdant oases of getting high!
Thanks for a future in which schools of silver-pink glinty fish
Beach themselves without saying why.

Through your power
Higher natures awaken.
The guys who worked at Higher Path,
The local pot store, got shot
During a robbery.
Sweet long-haired dudes,
Both killed.

Congrats on being invisible!

Maybe you felt disrespected
By my grumbling last night,
Or during the infamous "London Meltdown"
(An oft-visited exhibit in my private hall of humiliation)
From which I'm still recovering. But no!
Those unhappy lapses were
Mere blips of primordial chaos,
Evil inquisitors within, adverse reactions
To current events, or the medicine's simply not

Working again. Yet you made me
The cracked thing I am! Gave me mockery
For a middle name! (I talk about everyone like that
When I'm mad. Don't pretend you're devastated.)

Today a man said to me,
Be nice to his penis . . . A friendly enough sentiment,
Yet I hung my head and was ashamed.

Lord, can you rally whatever's left?
Chaff and dregs and sloppy grounds
At the bottom of the pot? Let the Druze
Religion be true: may reincarnation represent
The cosmos's central mechanism! Lasting spirit,
Spare me. I require more time prior to the dread
Moment of impact, the inevitable, half-
Remembered, half-imagined shutdown! Wow!

Page 37 The poem "Early Greek Philosophy" draws on information in the excellent book *Early Greek Philosophy*, translated and edited by Jonathan Barnes. (Betty Radice, Advisory ed. 2nd rev. ed. New York: Penguin Books, 2001.)

Page 52 The end of the poem "On the Idea the Dead May Live Vicariously Through Us" makes use of a quote from Ecclesiastes 1:2–4:

> [2] Vapor of vapors *and* futility of futilities! All is vanity.
>
> [3] What profit does man have left from all his toil at which he toils under the sun?
>
> [4] One generation goes and another generation comes, but the earth remains forever.

Page 66 The image at the end of "Miraculous," is slightly bent but nonetheless lifted from Walter Benjamin's writings on his drug experiences. (Howard Eiland, ed. *On Hashish*. Cambridge, MA: Belknap Press, 2006.)

PHOTO BY BENJAMIN WEISSMAN

Amy Gerstler is a writer of poetry, nonfiction, and journalism. Her book *Dearest Creature* (Penguin 2009) was named a *New York Times* Notable Book and was short-listed for the Los Angeles Times Book Prize in Poetry. Her previous twelve books include *Ghost Girl, Medicine, Crown of Weeds*, which won a California Book Award, *Nerve Storm*, and *Bitter Angel*, which won a National Book Critics Circle Award in poetry. She was the 2010 guest editor of the yearly anthology *The Best American Poetry*. Her work has appeared in a variety of magazines and anthologies, including *The New Yorker, The Paris Review, The American Poetry Review, Poetry*, several volumes of *The Best American Poetry*, and *Postmodern American Poetry: A Norton Anthology*. She has taught writing and/or visual art at the California Institute of the Arts, Caltech, Art Center College of Design, the University of Utah, Pitzer College, the writing seminars at Bennington College, and elsewhere. She currently teaches in the MFA Writing Program at the University of California, Irvine.